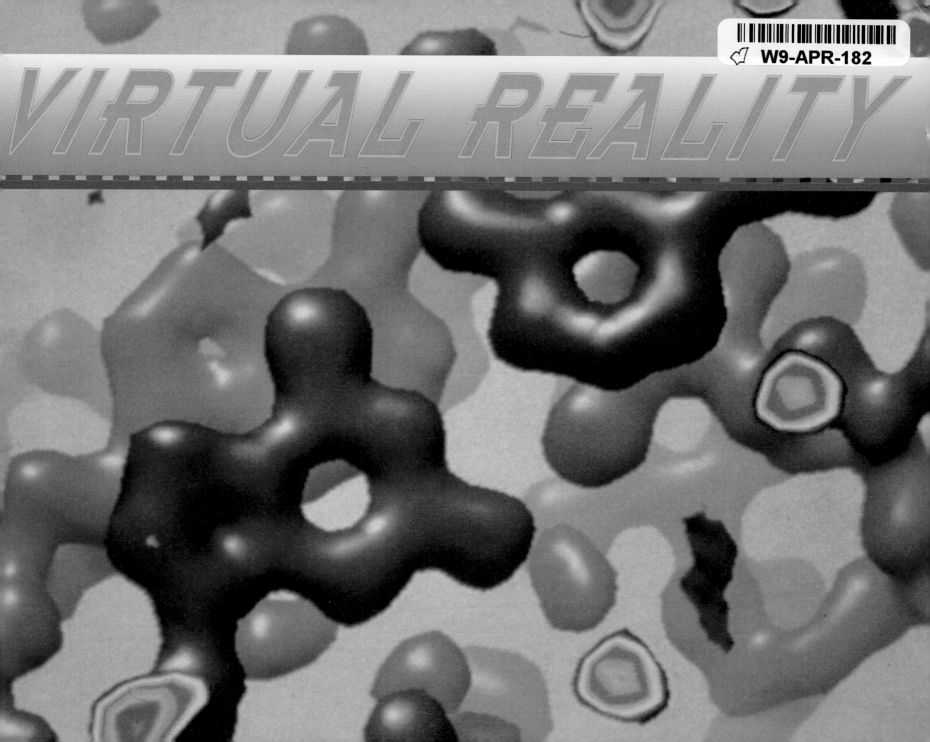

VIRTUAL REALITY

VIRTUAL REALITY

by HP NEWQUIST

A Byron Preiss Book
Scholastic Inc.
New York

Cover design and photoshop illustration by Heidi North.
Cover photographs: Inset, courtesy Evans and Sutherland™; border and backround of DNA molecules courtesy the Scripps Research Institute.

Interior Photographs:
Title page: Scripps Research Institute; p. 10: Vituality—altered on computer by Dimitry Kushnirsky; p. 11, 13, 20, 21, 30: Evans & Sutherland™; p. 12, 14-15, 27, 40, 58, 74, 77, 78, 81, 82: The Vivid Group; p. 16: courtesy of Exxon Corporation and Pacific Data Images; p. 17: United States Air Force Museum; p. 18, 29 (bottom left, upper and bottom right), 76: Division Limited; p. 19: courtesy of Evans & Sutherland™—rendered in 3-D by Gerald Marks; p. 22: courtesy of CAE-Link Corp./Binghamton, NY; p. 23: © Disney/Lucasfilm Ltd.; p. 24: Illustration by Heidi North; p. 25, 26, 41: Envision and photoshop illustration by Heidi North; p. 28, 53: VRI; p. 29 (center), 54, 55: courtesy of Medical Media Systems and Silicon Graphics; p. 29 (upper left), 43: Virtuality; p. 32-33, 37, 42: NASA; p. 35: courtesy of StrayLight Corp., Warren NJ; p. 36, 64, 65, 67: Sprint; p. 39, 45: courtesy of Byron Preiss Multimedia—rendered in 3-D by Gerald Marks; p. 44, 48: Bill Jepson/UCLA; p. 46: University of North Carolina at Chapel Hill, Department of Computer Science/photo by Bo Strain; p. 47, 59: courtesy of Virtus Corporation—rendered in 3-D by Gerald Marks; p. 49: Division & ATMA; p. 50-51, 56: VPL Research; p. 52: courtesy Abington Memorial Hospital; p. 57: courtesy of the Scripps Research Institute—rendered in 3-D by Gerald Marks; p. 61: AP/Wide World Photos; p. 63: courtesy of Sense8/Temple of Horus, created by Lynn Holden and Carl Loeffler/sponsored by Intel Corporation—rendered in 3-D by Gerald Marks; p. 68: Autodesk; p. 69, 72-73: courtesy of Volvo and Silicon Graphics; p. 71: image courtesy of Autodesk/created by Yann Bertaud with AutoCad™, AutoSurf™, AutoVision™—rendered in 3-D by Gerald Marks; p. 75: Corporate Communication Group; p. 79, 80: Myron W. Krueger, Artificial Reality, Vernon, CT; p. 83: rendered in 3-D by Gerald Marks on BRYCE software; p. 84: Sense8; p. 85: courtesy of Amusitronix—rendered in 3-D by Gerald Marks; p. 90: photo by Trini Newquist—colorized by Heidi North; p. 91: photo by J. R. Rost.

Special thanks to Kate Waters, Jennifer Riggs, Cary Ryan, Joe Eagle, Li Bendet, Rachel Cooper, Nuri Celikgil, Mark Pressman, Ian Bryden, and Carl Goodman at the Museum of the Moving Image.
Editors: Kathy Huck and Wendy Wax
Assistant Editor: Robin Ambrosino
Book Design: Heidi North

Library of Congress Cataloging-in-Publication Data 95-9900

Newquist, HP (Harvey P.)
Virtual reality / by HP Newquist.
    p.   cm.
ISBN: 0-590-48408-7
1. Human-computer interaction. 2. Virtual reality.
1. Virtual reality. 2. Human-computer interaction.] I. Title.
QA76.9.H85N49   1995
006—dc20   95-9900
         CIP
         AC

12 11 10 9 8 7 6 5 4 3 2 1   7 8 9/9 0/0

Printed in the U.S.A.
First Scholastic printing, November 1995

Contents

Dear Reader,

For more than ten years I have written about many of the newest and most exciting technologies being developed throughout the world. These technologies range from the creation of thinking machines and "seeing" robots to the invention of computers so small that they can fit on the head of a pin.

Of all these fascinating advances, virtual reality, or VR as it is commonly termed, seems to me to have the greatest potential to significantly affect people's lives. VR is already being used by people in all walks of life, and in the years to come it will be used in homes and classrooms in the same way that computers and TVs are used today.

The reason that VR is so important is that it can take people to places they have never been and enable them to do things they never believed possible. In the following pages, you will read about the computers, headsets, gloves, flight simulators, and other components of VR that will someday change the way we live our lives.

VR will let you visit people in other parts of the world and make it seem as if they are as close as your next-door neighbors. It will let you explore other planets without ever leaving your bedroom. And it will let you be creative in ways that are limited only by your sense of adventure and your imagination. It is a technology—and a tool—that you can use tomorrow by reading about it today.

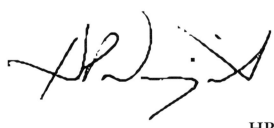

HP Newquist

There are ten illustrations in this book that you can see in three-dimension. On the page, they are flat and two-dimensional, but when you look through our specially designed glasses, the images look like they're coming right at you!

In order to understand how this process works, let's do an experiment: Choose one thing to focus on. First close only one eye and then only the other eye. Notice how the image seems to shift. With both eyes open, your brain compares the different information transmitted from your left and right eyes to give you a sense of depth, or three-dimensionality. A plane or surface, like a photograph, is only two-dimensional. It does not have depth. It is, however, possible to "fool" your eyes into believing that two-dimensional pictures have depth.

Experts have experimented with 3-D imaging for years. To successfully create the appearance of 3-D, the image first has to be altered and then to be viewed through colored glasses.

The lenses of these special glasses are made of translucent plastic. There is a red filter in the left lens and a blue-green filter in the right lens, which, although it appears to be blue, is a combination of blue and green.

Each 3-D illustration is comprised of two slightly shifted images of the same picture. Each image is rendered in a different color—one in red and one in blue-green. When the viewer looks at the illustrations through the special glasses, the left eye looks through the red filter, seeing only the blue-green image, while the right eye looks through the blue-green filter, seeing only the red image. This trick forces your eyes to get two separate pictures that are slightly different in perspective. This "binocular" vision is interpreted by the brain as three-dimensionality.

To maximize the 3-D experience, be sure to put your glasses on correctly. If you wear reading glasses, hold the 3-D glasses in front of your regular glasses.

Note: These ten 3-D illustrations were created to make you feel as if you are experiencing VR, yet you really aren't. The difference between VR and these images is that real VR simulations consist of moving images that change over a period of time. The illustrations in this book don't change. They do, however, show you what virtual reality would feel like at one moment, as if a VR moment were frozen in time. It is our way of bringing you as close as possible to the VR experience!

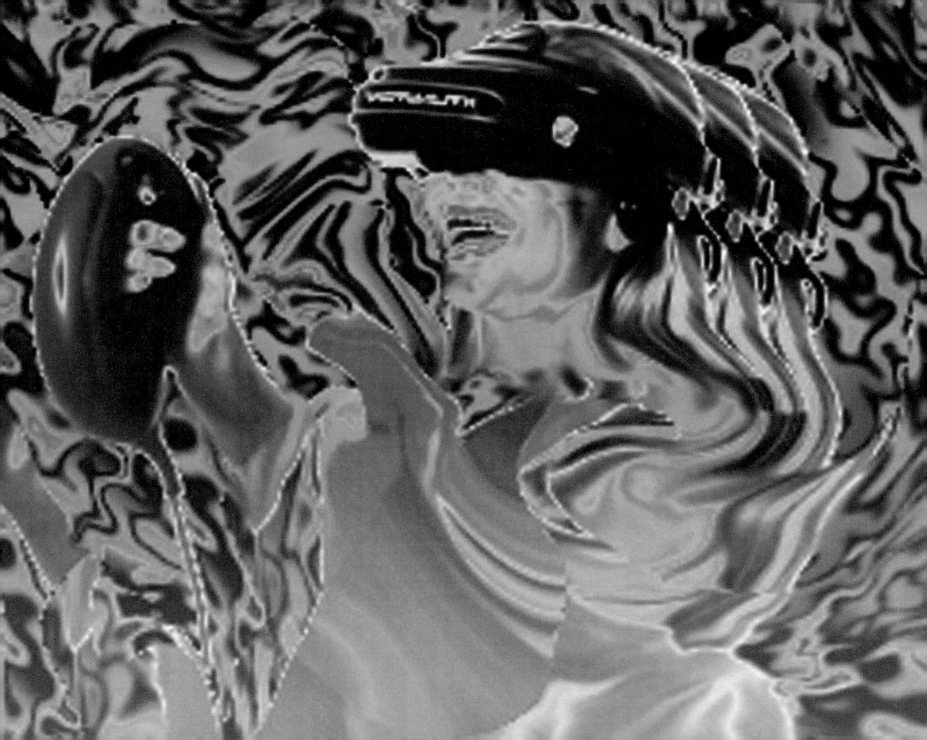

Chapter 1

Imagine

being *inside* your favorite video game. Not inside the actual machine, where all the wires and electrical components are, but inside the actual *game*, where the space ships, haunted houses, or street fighters are. If you were inside, you could sit in the spaceships, talk to the ghosts, or grab the gun out of the bad guy's hand. You could be part of the game, not just somebody watching it. Looking in every direction, you could feel just as if the game were happening in the real world.

This type of game actually exists. It's a new type of computer system called virtual reality, which can let you go *inside* a video world.

Watch out for Vermus the dragon in this video game!
←You can really get into virtual reality with the right gear, just like the girl in this composite illustration.

Virtual reality, known as VR, is the name for a place where everything you see and do is created by a computer. This computer is more than just a computer that hooks up to your TV and powers your video games. It is a computer that lets you enter into a virtual world where you can move around, touch things, and see characters and places that you would never see in your everyday life.

In real life you are able to look in every direction. Think about walking down the street near your home. No matter which direction you look in, you can always see something, whether it's the buildings nearby, the cars up ahead, the kids playing behind you, or the trees on both sides of the street. VR lets you have

As seen in this composite photo of a virtual hockey game, you can be a star goalie.

this same type of experience, but instead of walking through the real world you're walking through a video game world. It is not like looking at a regular computer or TV screen. In vir-

tual reality, you can look in front of you and behind you and up and down and all around, and everything you see is part of the computer game. You can move through the game along with the

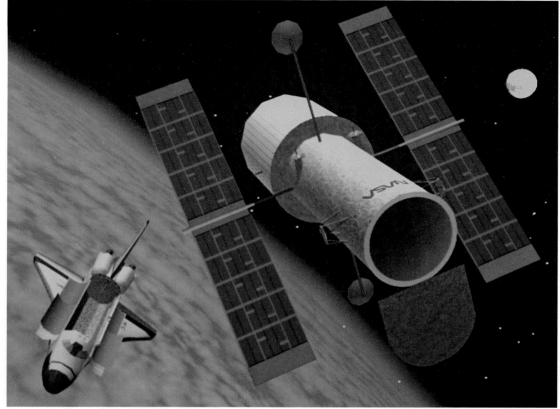

Data gathered by the Hubble telescope is later used in VR programs.

game's characters, which you no longer perceive as just little figures on the screen. Now *you* can see everything that they see from their perspective!

Real life is unpredictable. You never know exactly what is going to happen from one moment to the next. Real life is also limited. For one thing, you can only be in one place at any particular time. If you are in your classroom at school, for example, then you can't possibly be on the surface of the planet Mars or at the bottom of a volcano. For another thing, there are places that you can't go in real life. Even if you wanted to, you couldn't go to Mars or the bottom of a volcano. People haven't yet learned how to get to such places, and even if they had, they wouldn't be able to survive there. The warmest day on Mars is a bone-chilling 20 degrees below zero, and the bottom of a volcano reaches temperatures of more than 1000 degrees—hot enough to melt your family car down to a puddle of liquid metal in seconds.

HERE'S HOW VIRTUAL REALITY DIFFERS FROM REAL LIFE:

- **It allows you to control things that happen around you.**
- **It enables you, at least seemingly, to be in two different places at once.**
- **It enables you to go to places you couldn't get to in real life—sometimes places so dangerous you wouldn't even think about visiting them.**

Thanks to the power of computers and VR software and equipment, you can enter a world where many things are possible.

People have been doing VR for years now. In the following chapters you'll find out how VR has been used in the past and how it will be used in the future. But first we'll take a look at how the idea of virtual reality came into being.

The program "SharkBait" allows you to go places you normally wouldn't be able to go, like the ocean floor. This is a composite photograph.

Chapter 2

When Virtual Reality Began

The term

virtual reality was not actually used until the 1980s, but the idea of using computers to create other worlds has been discussed since the 1960s. Computers themselves have only been around since the 1950s, although it may seem as if they've been here forever. By the end of the 1960s computers were enabling people to draw pictures that looked almost like photographs. These pictures could be linked together to make short clips of animation that looked more real than cartoons or other hand-drawn films and were cheaper to make. Unlike cartoons or real movies, where the action is filmed and recorded and cannot be easily changed, a computer can keep an animation in its memory. Because of this, animations can be changed

A car turns into a tiger by "morphing," or fading of one image into another.

quickly and simply by reprogramming parts of the computer program. A car could be changed to a tiger, for instance, with very little work, and the viewer could see the changes right away. To make a change like this in a movie, the actors and film crew would have to refilm the entire scene with a tiger.

A Virtual Idea Is Born

In the late 1960s, the United States military decided it needed to find a way to train pilots to use its jet fighters. While the pilots already knew how to fly jets, they were not familiar with the complex systems that were involved in flying the world's fastest planes or deploying the weapons they carried. Since one wrong move on the part of the

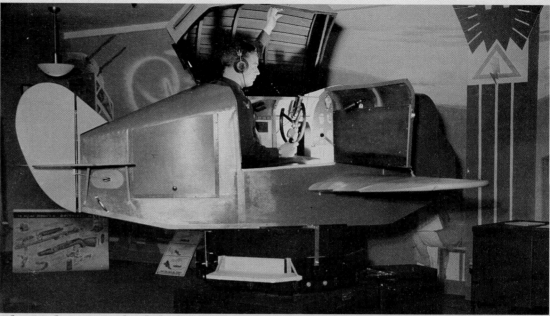

The Link trainer, built before World War I, was one of the first flight simulators used to train pilots.

pilot might result in a crash, it was too risky to send pilots up in the air with all this complicated machinery. In order to train its pilots, the military began to think about using computers to simulate the cockpit of a jet fighter. This means they created realistic pictures of the cockpit on the computer screen.

The idea of being able to make such quick adjustments was very appealing to the military. It would make computer animation a suitable tool for giving pilots and soldiers a realistic idea

Soldiers can train for ground fighting in a VR simulation.

feel as if they were involved in what was happening on the screen.

A Need for Immersion

Researchers working on computer simulation knew that the aspect of simulation that was missing was something known as immersion. Immersion is the word we use when we talk about getting into a swimming pool or a bathtub: We immerse ourselves in the water. It is also used by businesspeople when they talk about their work; they say they are immersed in their work when they are thinking only about their jobs and nothing else. If you play a musical instrument and you immerse

Watch out! You have three jet fighters coming right at you! →

of what they could expect when they went into combat.

The use of computer animation to create a simulated environment became known as computer simulation. Computers could generate scenes that looked real enough to give people an idea of what they might see in real life. But, like movies and cartoons, computer simulations still didn't convince viewers that they were actually part of the action. Something was missing that would make viewers

An air force trainee tests his skill in a virtual F16 cockpit.

tricking the viewer's senses into accepting virtual or computer generated images and sounds as part of the real world. Of course, this meant replacing normal sights and sounds with computer-generated sights and sounds. The first efforts to do this resulted in "wraparound" movie theaters the size of an airplane cockpit. The pilots sat inside these simulators and watched computer-generated movies, oblivious to what was happening in the real world.

The First VR Systems

yourself in practicing, you are not thinking about anything except your lesson. You have immersed yourself in your music.

Researchers realized that simulation could not be completely realistic unless the people watching the simulation were immersed in the same world as the simulation. Only if people were immersed in the simulation could it be used to recreate real-life situations. But how could this be done?

It could be done by making the viewer's subconscious believe that it was in a different world. And this could only be done by

The rest, as they say, is history. The first system that used VR technology was called the Virtual Cockpit. Similar to the arcade and mall games where you sit in the seat of a race car or a jet fighter, the Virtual Cockpit allowed pilots to pretend they were flying an airplane with-

A trainee practices his takeoff through immersion.

out ever leaving the ground. A real cockpit was constructed on moving platforms which simulated the movement of a jet. The cockpit was enclosed so that the pilots could not see out of it, and the only images they saw were those projected on their windows by a computer. Whenever the pilots moved the control stick—which normally would have controlled the wing flaps on an airplane—the moving platform would tilt the cockpit in the proper manner, giving the pilots the feeling that they were controlling a real airplane. They could practice landings and take-

Stilts allow the Chinook simulator to move like an airborne helicopter without the dangers of crashing.

offs and even dogfights in midair without worrying about crashing. When they became skilled at operating the simulator, these pilots could then go out and fly real jets with confidence.

New and Improved Virtual Reality

Eventually researchers shrank the enclosed cockpit down to the size of a helmet. Since pilots and soldiers already wore helmets and often used headphones and headsets, researchers used modified versions of these devices to further immerse their wearers in virtual worlds. And, as it turned out, simulation was much more effective when each person could control his or her own VR world instead of having to share it in a movie-style setting. Movie-style immersion is still very popular, though, and is used in many amusement park attractions

Viewers participate in the 3-D Star Tours ride at Walt Disney World.

fast-moving action on a huge movie screen makes them feel as if they were traveling forward through space.

This type of VR, still referred to as simulation, is the kind of VR that most of us will use or experience during the next few years. Why? Because it's less expensive than some of the more complex forms of VR, which can cost as much as a house. The cost is so high because the VR gear that you wear and the computers that control it are very expensive to manufacture. Over the next few years, however, prices will come down to the point where everyone can afford to use VR. Then it will show up in businesses and homes and maybe even your classroom. That's when you'll get to be in two places at once—or at least feel as if you are.

Now we'll see exactly how you, too, can enter into the VR world.

throughout the world, such as Star Tours at Disneyland and Walt Disney World and the Back to the Future Ride at Universal Studios. In these rides people sit in a small room or compartment and travel to other planets and strange places while their seats move up and down and rock back and forth. All the while,

Making Sense of What's Real

Chapter 3

In the real world, the one in which you live every day,

your senses make you aware of the things around you and the things that happen to you. Your connection to the world depends on your ability to use these senses—sight, hearing, touch, taste, and smell—as your guides. Let's take something as simple as playing baseball. Imagine that you are playing in the outfield. Your job is to catch the ball when it comes toward you or at least to get it fast enough to throw it back to a player covering one of the bases.

Using Your Senses on the Playing Field

Think about what happens when you are out in the field. You are watching the pitcher throw the ball to the batter, and you are also listening to the other players on your team as they talk during the game. One of your hands is in a baseball glove while the other is free to grab the ball and throw it. As you watch, you see the ball leave the pitcher's hand and head toward the batter. Then you see the batter swing, and you hear the sound of the ball hitting the bat. You see the ball sail over the pitcher's head and fly up into the air. Even though the ball is only a white speck, your eyes lock onto it and follow it as it makes its way toward you. You think about where the ball is heading, and you begin to run to where you believe it will land.

Sight, touch, and hearing are valuable senses in a baseball game.

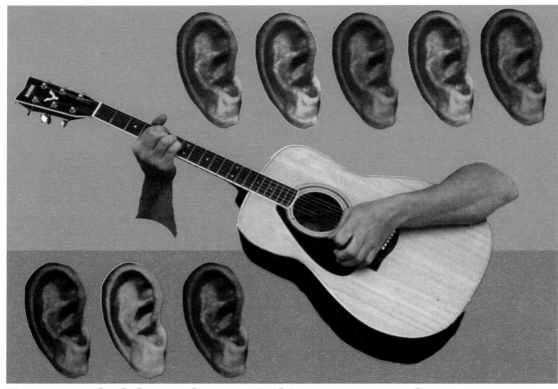

Your senses also help you play a musical instrument correctly.

As you move, you hold out your glove to get ready to catch the ball. You yell "Got it!" to your teammates so that no one will collide with you and make you miss the ball. They are also yelling for you to hurry up and get the ball back to first base. As you watch the ball drop from the sky, you lift your glove to the place where your eyes and your mind tell you the ball will end up. If everything goes as it should, you hear the satisfying *smack* of the ball as it lands in your glove. Then you quickly grab the ball out of the glove with your other hand and look to see where the batter has run to. If he or she has run past first, your teammates are probably yelling "Second base! Second base!" You make a quick decision and hurl the ball to second base, where you hope the runner will be tagged out. You can only hope, of course, because in the real world it is often difficult to predict whether or not something will happen. Sometimes things work out; sometimes they don't.

While playing ball, you use three of your five senses: sight, hearing, and touch. You watch the ball, you hear the sound of the bat and the sound of your teammates' voices, and you touch the ball and grasp it when you throw it back to the infield. You don't use your senses of taste or smell—unless you end up sliding into home and get a mouthful of dirt or smell the grass on the field. Taste and smell are important for some activities, especially eating, but they don't play as important a role in our daily lives as sight, hearing, and touch.

Using Your Senses in Other Ways

Playing baseball is only one example of how you use your senses. Your senses also help you perform tasks or take part in activities such as playing music. If you play guitar or piano, for example, you must use your eyes to watch your instrument (sense of sight) so that you can guide your fingers over the neck of the guitar or the piano keyboard (sense of touch). You can tell if you're playing correctly by listening to the sound of the instrument (sense of hearing) as your fingers press the guitar strings or piano keys. If you make a mistake, your sense of hearing tells you to

You can trick your senses by playing virtual golf, as in this composite photograph.

make a correction, and this information is fed back to your eyes by the brain so that they can guide your fingers to the proper positions.

Your senses also work together to help you get dressed, get on the school bus, do your classwork, eat your lunch, do your homework, watch TV, listen to the stereo, and get ready for bed at night. Your senses are your link to the world in which you live.

Your senses are as important

in the world of virtual reality as they are in the real world. In fact, as we have seen, virtual reality depends on a computer's ability to trick your senses into convincing you that you are in a different world. VR has to create an illusion that makes you believe you are experiencing something that isn't really there—a virtual world that exists only inside a computer. VR does this by using special equipment that links your senses right into the computer.

Chapter 4

Virtual Reality Equipment

Most

activities and games require that you use some special equipment. For video games you need a joystick, a video monitor, and software. For music you need an instrument. For football you need a helmet, padding, and a ball. When you read or write, you need a book, or paper and a pen—or maybe you write on a computer, which means that you use a monitor and a keyboard. Even when you're doing something as simple as watching a movie, the screen and the film are part of the equipment. Creating virtual reality requires extremely complicated equipment, such as special helmets, gloves, computers, and even body suits.

This futuristic-looking helmet is actually a VR headpiece.

This is a collage of the gadgets which together make VR realistic (clockwise, starting from the top): headpiece, computer with audio cord, joystick, seated simulator, and computer screen.

The VR Headpiece

The first thing you do to enter a virtual world is put on a helmet—a headpiece that looks like something the centurions wear in the movie *Star Wars*. It is the job of this helmet to provide your senses with all the information they need to make you believe that you are someplace else. Just as you used your eyes and ears to watch and then catch the baseball, the VR system uses your eyes and ears to guide you through the activities in a virtual world.

The helmet, also called a headpiece or a head-mounted display, fits snugly over your face and ears, much like a football helmet with a face mask. The face mask keeps you from seeing

With the helmet on you feel like you're in a completely different environment.

anything around you in the real world. Inside the helmet there is a special set of glasses which are similar to the eyepieces of binoculars. But while binoculars let you view what's actually in front of you, the eyepieces in the helmet let you look into an entirely different world, a video world that is created by the software that is in the memory of a computer. Each of these eyepieces is a mini computer screen that plays the computer-generated video in 3-D. Since the helmet covers your head, you see nothing except the pictures inside your eyepieces. They fill up your entire field of vision. Everything you see is generated by the computer. The computer even controls your peripheral vision—the vision you use when you look out of the corner of your eyes. Usually, when you look at a video game, you can still see some things in your peripheral vision,

such as people standing nearby. This keeps you aware of your surroundings. With the VR helmet, your peripheral vision is completely blocked, so you don't see anything around you that reminds you of where you actually are.

The helmet is also equipped with powerful high-tech headphones. They are like regular headphones except for one thing: They push sound into your ears from all directions. Following instructions from the computer, these headphones make sounds that seem to come from above you, behind you, and even under you. Since the computer controls both the headphones and the eyepieces in your helmet, you might hear something flying over your head and then look up and see the object that is making the sound—as if it were flying across the ceiling of the room you're in. With these headphones you hear only the things that are part of your vir-

tual world. You don't hear sounds from the real world—people calling, cars driving by, a television blaring. Everything you hear comes from the world that you see in the computer eyepieces of your helmet.

The last thing that makes the helmet work is a small tracking device that tells the computer where you are looking. This tracking device monitors the position of your head and relays this information to the computer. Acting like a compass, it can determine whether you turn your head left or right, up or down. If you look up, for example, the computer knows to change the video scene to a view of what you might see above you. Because the computer is getting feedback from the tracking device, you are able to look all the way around you and see a complete world. In order to be realistic, the video scenes generated in your helmet must change when you look in different directions just as they would in the real world. If the computer did not have a tracking device, you would just be looking at the same picture from different angles, which is a lot like looking at the corners of a TV screen. Seeing in VR is quite a bit different from looking at a video game, where the scene on the screen is all that you see. If you look away from the screen in a video game, you don't see the game anymore: Instead, you might see your friends or other people standing around. But in VR games, when you look around, you still see the action of the game—whether it's aliens chasing after you, a building that you have just left, or a basketball game in front of you.

The helmet takes care of your senses of sight and hearing, but the sense of touch is important in the real world, too. Astonishingly enough, VR technology can also bring your sense of touch into the virtual world with a specialized glove called a dataglove.

The Dataglove

The dataglove is outfitted with little sensors and wires that send signals back to the computer, just like the compass device on the helmet. The wires relay detailed information about the way you move your hand and fingers. This means that the computer can tell if you are making a fist or pointing at an object—or trying to grab hold of something you see in your helmet.

Why is it necessary for the computer to know what your hand is doing? Well, when you are using VR, you can't see your own hand because the helmet is covering your eyes. By using the information conveyed by

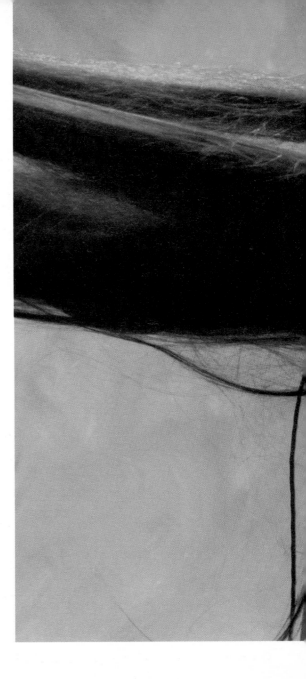

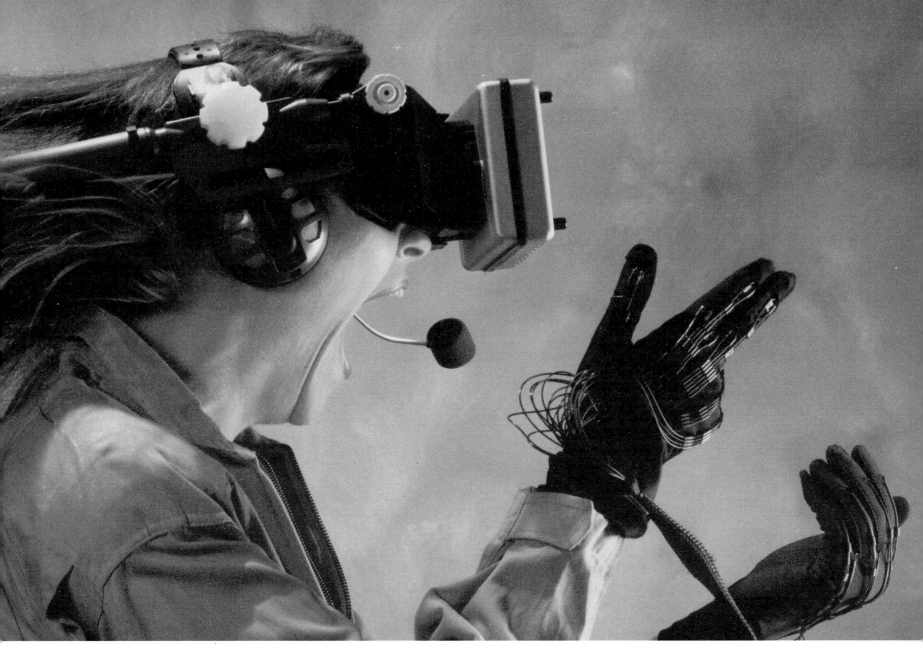

Datagloves, in addition to the headpiece, increase the immersion effect.

the dataglove, the computer can create a picture of your hand for you to see inside the helmet. This computerized hand, which looks like the hand of a robot, will do everything that your real hand will do: point, touch, wave, and even grab things. So, even though you can't see your real hand because of your helmet, the computer feeds your eyepieces an animated version of your hand that lets you see what your hand is doing as you move through your virtual world. Hold your hand up in front of your helmet, and a computerized picture of your hand shows up right in front of your eyes. While you yourself cannot actually touch the objects the computer is generating, your "virtual" hand can.

Being able to see a part of yourself—your hand—in the virtual world heightens the illusion that you are actually in the place created by the computer. You are seeing a part of yourself in the scene, just as you do in real life when you put out your hand to grab the handlebars of a bicycle or push an elevator button.

All Geared Up

With all this equipment on, you look something like an astronaut. The real world, the one which you can no longer see or hear, is gone for the time being. You are now in a different world—one that *you* have chosen—one where all your experiences are created by the computer. And in this new computer world you can hunt dinosaurs in a forest, fly a spaceship over the moon's surface, drive race cars on the ocean floor, or even shrink yourself down to the size of a fly and buzz through the rooms of a castle. You will be able to grab stars, lift up tanks, and push holes through mountains. And you will never have to leave the room to do it.

By now you might think VR sounds great, a wonderful way of putting yourself into strange video games and exploring unusual worlds. And it is. But virtual reality is more than the world's greatest toy. It is something people are already using to help them explore outer space, investigate the microscopic world, and walk through buildings before they are ever built. Despite its entertainment value, VR technology is taken very seriously by scientists and businesspeople all around the world. Let's look at how these people are currently using VR and then see how you might use VR in the future.

The CyberTron™ is a three-dimensional cage for a whole body experience. →

34

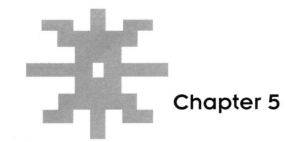

Chapter 5

Scientists and Invisible Worlds

Whether

you are a scientist or a kid participating in virtual reality, the gear and the equipment remain the same. It is the computer's software that allows people to use VR for different things. It is the software—which can be found on a floppy disk or a game cartridge—that actually creates the street fighters, aliens, and planets of the virtual world.

There are many kinds of software. When you play video games, you are using software. The software on one game cartridge might have Mario Brothers™, while another piece of software might have Sonic the Hedgehog or a video boxing match. Other kinds of software let people write letters and books, while still others let people store their phone numbers and addresses.

A doctor studies a computerized X ray.

Obviously different software is good for different things.

The same is true of VR software. It can take many forms and create many realities, ranging from architecture to medical surgery to space exploration.

Seeing Air

Scientists are using virtual reality to see things that they can't normally see, like air. Air is invisible, but you know it is there because you can feel it when the wind blows. Air affects a lot of things, like the way airplanes and rockets fly and the way the weather changes. Since air is invisible, it is hard to tell how it is changing or what it is doing—how thick it is, for example, or how much of it is moving in a given direction. But in a VR world, scientists can make the air visible by giving it color. They can then see how the air moves over the wing of a plane or how it moves when it turns into a tornado. They do this by putting on the same equipment—a helmet and a dataglove—that allows you to go into a VR video game, except that they do it in order to watch a computer simulation of air currents.

Visiting Planets

Going a step further, scientists can also study the atmospheres and weather on other planets without ever getting into a rocket. For many years satellites traveling

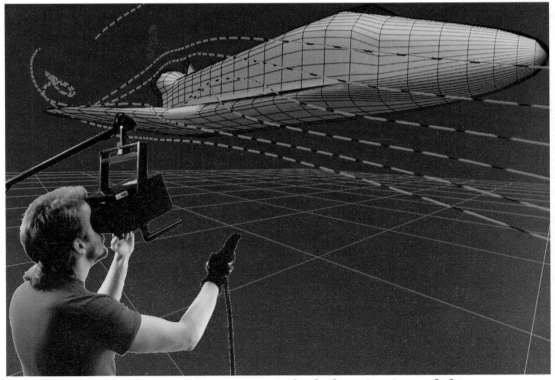

In this composite photograph you can see both the scientist and the NASA–Ames Virtual Windtunnel he is observing.

around Mars and Jupiter have been sending information back to Earth about the conditions on these planets. But this information is in the form of mathematical data that consists of hundreds of thousands of numbers printed on many pages of paper. Using VR, programmers can produce software that will read this data and convert it into a video of what the planet's atmosphere actually looks like. For scientists this is like being put into their own video game, but here it's a game of exploring and picking up clues about *real* planets instead of searching for magic flags or hidden treasures.

Stepping Into a Microscopic Universe

While outer space is a difficult place to get to in the real world, it is just as hard for scientists to examine and explore the microscopic world that is around us. Atoms, molecules, cells—a whole universe of unseen particles and organisms—float around and even into us at every moment of the day. The only way we can see how they look and act is to view them through a microscope. But many particles are so small that it is difficult to see them through even the most powerful microscopes. Scientists know what they look like and how they behave, but they have a hard time trying to watch them.

But, once again, VR comes to the rescue. There is now a kind of software that describes how atoms and molecules move around and how they connect with one another. Using this software, scientists can create virtual worlds where these particles appear big enough to hold in the palms of their hands. Inside the VR world, they can grab particular atoms or molecules and at-

tach them to other atoms or molecules to see if they will join together to form new compounds. When scientists find connections between atoms and molecules in the virtual world, they can go back to their labs and create these new substances in the real world. In this way, they can produce new chemicals and medicines far more quickly than they could without the aid of VR.

These are all areas of science in which VR is proving to be a valuable tool for research and exploration. Yet, to make these virtual journeys even more successful, VR developers are concentrating on one aspect of our real world that we take almost for granted: the world of touch at the end of our fingertips.

A computer-created 3-D image of Venus. The data in the foreground tells us the viewer's distance from the mountain, the location of the mountain, and the altitude of the geographical area. →

Chapter 6

Reaching Out to the Unreal World

Fooling your fingers is one of the hardest obstacles for VR developers.

One

of the interesting things about VR that has come out of scientific research into microscopic worlds is the need to make data-gloves respond to levels of touch. While it might seem that this is not such a big deal, think about how important touch is to something as simple as throwing a ball. When you grab a ball to throw it, you apply a certain amount of pressure with your fingers in order to hold it tightly before throwing it. If the ball were an egg, though, you would grab it more gently and toss it with less force. You would also grab a ball differently than you'd grab a Frisbee because of the difference in their shapes.

In a virtual world, you may have the illusion that you are grabbing something because you see your hand reaching out for it and then grasping it. But, you aren't *really* grabbing anything. What you are grabbing is a *picture* of a molecule or a star or an alien's head. VR systems are trying to give users a sense of touch in their worlds, but it is harder to fool the nerves in your fingers than it is to fool your eyes and ears. Creating a real sense of touch in the virtual world has been very difficult to accomplish.

Fooling Your Fingers

There are a number of ways in which VR developers are trying to make your fingers feel as if they are actually grabbing virtual objects. The first way is by inserting tiny air

VR tries to recreate actual sensory experiences, like throwing a baseball.

In this composite photograph, a scientist at the NASA–Ames Research Center in Mountain View, California, inspects a virtual rock found at Mars Hill in Death Valley, three hundred miles away.

metal pads that press against various parts of your hand and fingers. Like the finger bags, the plastic or metal pads press with the appropriate amount of force, depending on what you are holding and how tightly you are squeezing it.

All this is very difficult to do. Touching—which we don't give even a second thought in our daily lives—presents one of the biggest obstacles to making VR seem truly real.

Virtual Sense of Movement

There is another human sense that we don't give much thought to, one which is also becoming an important part of VR. It is called the kinesthetic sense, which means the sense of movement. Liquids and small hairs are in our bodies and our brains as well as in parts of our muscles. They tell us that

bags in the fingers of datagloves. When you place your fingers on a virtual object, the computer—which is monitoring the position of your hand—inflates the bags with small amounts of air to create the sensation of pressure. When you squeeze your fingers around a virtual meteorite, for example, the dataglove finger bags inflate with more air than if you grab a crystal vase, which you would handle more gently. Another way VR developers are doing this is by equipping the dataglove with tiny plastic or we are moving, even when we have our eyes closed or are not touching anything. Imagine yourself in a car, for example. Although you are sitting still and your feet are not moving or touching the ground, you still experience a sense of movement. If you close your eyes so that you don't see the passing scenes, you can still feel that you are moving. This is kinesthesis.

Some VR systems let you walk around in order to experience the sensation of moving, but you are usually limited by the length of the cables that connect your VR equipment to the computer. To get around this, VR developers often use a treadmill. Treadmills are exercise machines that let people walk or run for miles without ever leaving the room. This is possible because the treadmill platform has a moving surface that goes in the opposite direction of the walker. (You can experience this for yourself by trying to walk up an escalator that is going down: Unless you run really fast, you won't move forward at all.) If you are wearing a VR suit and walking on a treadmill, you can get the sensation of walking around.

All these technologies help to make VR more realistic. It is certain that in the coming years, researchers will find still other ways to make VR a more believable experience. These will involve making the equipment smaller and lighter so that you barely notice that you have it on, as well as making the computer-generated images look more like the real world.

Developers continue to improve the real-life experience of VR. These machines—Virtuality 1000 SD models—are used for seated simulations.

Chapter 7

Virtual Architecture

Being

able to move around in a virtual world has already proven to be extremely valuable in the field of architecture. For years houses and skyscrapers existed only on paper before they were built. Architectural drawings are very difficult to understand, and many can only be understood by trained professionals. To make these plans easier to understand, small models are often built to show what these structures will look like. Because of their tiny size, however, you can't walk around inside these models. Until a building is finished, no one really knows exactly what it will feel like to be inside it.

Often, after a building is finished, the architects or the people who live or work in the building wish they had done something different—put in more windows or made the hallways wider, for example. But by that time it is too late to make changes.

A virtual downtown Santa Monica, California, created by UCLA planners.

A 3-D recreation of Frank Lloyd Wright's Larkin Building. The original structure was built in Buffalo, New York, but torn down in 1937. →

Building Virtual Buildings

The University of North Carolina was in just such a predicament. The university was constructing a new building on campus and wanted to make sure that it was exactly right for its purposes. After an architectural firm designed the building, researchers created a virtual model of the building based on the architectural plans. Using VR gear and a treadmill, they then walked through the virtual building and found that they did in-

The actual interior of the lobby after construction in 1987.

The virtual interior of the lobby of Sitterson Hall at the University of North Carolina.

deed want more windows and bigger hallways. When they told the architects they wanted these changes, the architects said that there were already enough windows and that the hallways were wide enough. They believed this because they had worked only with the drawings. But when the researchers took the architects on a tour of the building as it existed in the VR system, the architects realized that the researchers were right about the building's design. They agreed to widen the halls

A 3-D virtual White House. The MAC™ window gives you a sense of viewing it on screen. →

The White House:Walk View

Widen a lane, add a traffic light. . . . UCLA planners can use VR to design roads and intersections.

and add more windows. If they had not been able to experience what the building would be like even before the foundation was put into place, the actual space would not have turned out as the university wanted. VR allowed the architects to make the build-ing more suitable to the needs of the people who had to work in it.

Virtual Home Improvement

VR doesn't apply only to big buildings. It can be used to experience the interi-ors of people's homes as well. With VR, for instance, shoppers can match appliances to specific sites in their homes before buying them. In Japan, where many peo-ple live in very small apartments, people use VR to be sure a new appliance such as a refrigerator will fit in an apartment. A shopper can bring drawings and a floor plan showing the size and layout of his or her kitchen to a special department store. The drawings and floor plans are entered into a VR system, and a virtual copy of the kitchen is created. The shopper can then try out different refrigerators in different sizes and colors and get a good sense of how they would look in his or her kitchen. This way, he or she can make sure the refrigerator is right before it is delivered.

Designing or remodeling a kitchen is a lot easier with VR.

Rebuilding Cities With VR

Many buildings, even entire cities, can be improved through the use of VR. After the fires, earthquakes, and riots in Los Angeles in the early 1990s, the people responsible for rebuilding the structures that had been destroyed chose to use VR to help them plan the city's new buildings and roadways.

Normally, city officials use small models of structures to give people an idea of what the builders have in mind. However, Los Angeles is one of the largest cities in the world, covering hundreds of square miles, and the hundreds of models that would have been needed would have been very expensive to build.

Instead of models and drawings, Los Angeles city planners created a VR world that is a replica of the city. This virtual Los Angeles is being used to show people how their neighborhoods are going to be rebuilt. In the virtual Los Angeles world,

This is a model of the German subway system rebuilt with the help of VR.

they can swoop down over the city as if they were in a plane or a helicopter and view the buildings from above. They can also go down specific streets to look at the actual buildings that are being rebuilt. In areas where there was complete destruction they can see where new buildings will be put, what kinds of buildings they will be, and how they will look in their setting. It's only a matter of adding a convenience store, a gas station, or a department store to the VR software. If the viewers aren't satisfied, the buildings can easily be changed or removed.

Designing Underground

VR has also proven its usefulness *beneath* the buildings of a city. When the Berlin Wall came down several years ago, allowing for a reunited Germany, it meant that people could travel freely between the two parts of Berlin. This was something that had not been possible for more than forty years. When East Berlin and West Berlin decided to reconnect their subways, which had also been separated for decades, they planned to join the two systems by combining two separate stations into a single station which would serve as a connection point.

The designers built a virtual model of the new station. The designers and builders were then able to walk through the planned station and make changes that would give it the appearance of one big station rather than two stations that had been joined together. VR provided a complete picture of what the station would ultimately look like before construction had even begun.

Chapter 8

Doctors and the World Under Our Skin

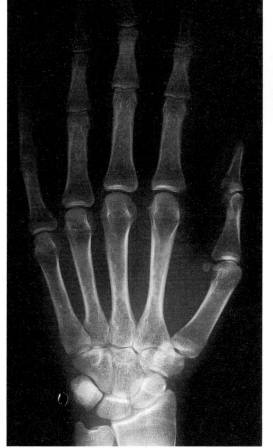

X rays are limited in what they can show of the human body.

The world under a person's skin holds thousands and thousands of secrets. Yet despite all the medical technology in existence today, including X rays and computer-generated images, there are no instruments that let a doctor look directly at a person's insides. Many devices, including tiny cameras, are used to take pictures and even movies of certain organs and body cavities, but they cannot give a wide view of large areas such as the chest and the abdomen. So, unless a doctor is making surgical cuts, it is not possible to see a cross section of the muscles, tissues, organs, and bones that are inside the human body. However, by using VR technology, a computer can create pictures of what is happening inside a body. To avoid unnecessary surgery, and to learn more about the human body, doctors are using virtual reality to "see" under people's skin.

Practice and Test Runs on Virtual Patients

Surgeons perform some of the most delicate and difficult procedures imaginable. And since each operation involves the health of a person, there is little room for error. Before they operate on real patients, surgeons can practice their surgical techniques or do test runs of complicated operations on virtual patients. Wearing VR gear, they can see a virtual patient through their headsets. The virtual patient is like a real person—with skin, hair, internal organs, a beating heart, and breathing lungs—only it is created by software.

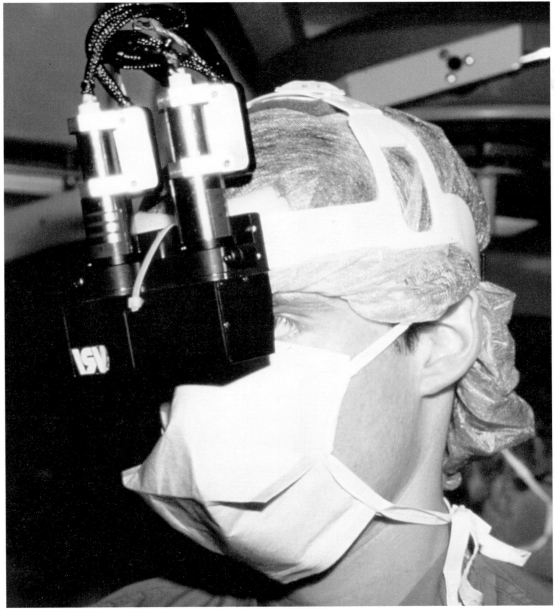

A doctor trains with VR gear before he operates on a real patient.

A close-up of a virtual knee.

ture at a time. They can't view the bones and muscles of the wrist in motion.

By outfitting the patient with a dataglove and monitoring how the healed hand moves, doctors can create an actual video of what is happening under that person's skin. In this case, the electronics on the glove create images on a video monitor instead of inside a helmet. The hand movements are tracked so that doctors can see where every bone and muscle is located, how well they have mended, and how well they are able to move.

VR Does What X rays Can't

VR is used for more than just surgical practice and preparation—it is also used to check the condition of a patient. When a person breaks a wrist, doctors can see the break by using X rays. Looking at X rays helps them to reset the bone. But once the bone has healed, it is hard to tell whether it has set properly, or whether the person can move his or her hand and fingers as easily as he or she did before it was broken. Doctors can't peel back the flesh to determine these things. And with X rays they are limited to taking only one pic-

"Watching" Medicine Work

Doctors at Loma Linda Hospital in California are using this same technique to treat patients with Parkinson's disease, a condition which causes sufferers to shake uncontrollably. Although this dis-

A doctor uses a computerized tracking device to locate a patient's ligament.

medicine is working the way it is supposed to.

While this is not an example of entering a virtual world, it does show how the tools of VR can be used for things other than simply going to places where no one has gone before. But doctors and researchers *do* want to use VR to go where no one has gone before: They want to walk through the human body.

A Tour of the Human Body

One of the drawbacks of learning anatomy by dissecting cadavers is that the human organs are relatively small. The heart is only about as big as a fist. The brain is about the size of two fists. The blood vessels are sometimes as thin as a single strand of hair, and

ease can be treated with medication, it has always been hard to tell exactly how well the medicine was working because there was no way to measure small decreases or increases in shaking. There were simply no instruments that could do this. But placing a dataglove on a patient's hand has allowed doctors to measure the amount of shaking in the hand. Using VR software, a precise tracking mechanism monitors the signals from the glove's sensors. Doctors can then measure the movement of the hand and decide whether the

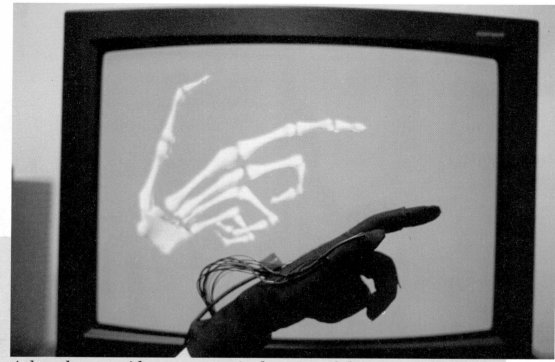
A dataglove provides a computerized version of the wearer's hand.

By entering this virtual body, students can more fully understand what goes on inside the real human body. They can enter the chambers of the heart to watch how blood flows through them, or they can stand in the outer ear and watch the movements of the inner ear as it responds to different types of sound. In real life this could never happen.

The last two chapters have dealt with VR simulations of environments that are too difficult to work with in real life, either because they are too small (like molecules) or too complicated (like unbuilt buildings). There are, however, times when VR can assist people with simple jobs and routines by letting them do something they could never do in real life: be in two places at once.

there are thousands of miles of them in the body. The small size of these organs makes it difficult for medical students to examine them. They must rely on oversized models of the heart, lungs, stomach, and so on to get an understanding of their structure and function.

VR is helping medical students look into the human body without cutting into a real one. Researchers have developed software that can produce a VR model of the inside of a human body. And, like the molecules mentioned earlier, this virtual body is so big that it seems as if the student has shrunk to the size of an insect.

A DNA molecule in 3-D. →

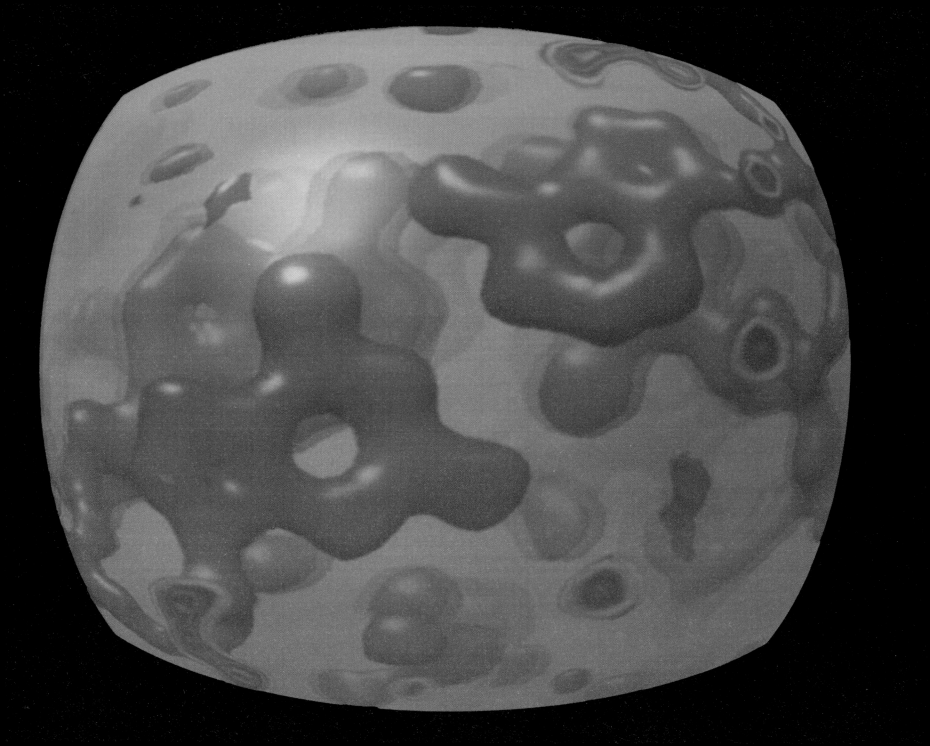

Chapter 9

Using VR to Explore Our World —and Other Worlds

You

know that you can't be in two places at once. It would be nice if you could, but it is impossible. Either you are here or you are there. You can't have it both ways—unless you are using VR.

VR creates the illusion that you are someplace other than where you actually are—on the surface of the moon, for example, or in an imaginary castle. You *know* that you aren't really in these places, but you are temporarily willing to believe that you are there.

As in this interactive project called "Virtual Cities," a student can plan cities of the future. This is a composite picture.

Stonehenge, the ancient circle of stones in England, in 3-D.→

Suspension of Disbelief

The term for believing in something you know isn't true is *suspension of disbelief.* As a phrase, it may sound strange and not make much sense, but all the VR professionals use it, so you should become familiar with it as well.

Movies and videos make you believe in characters and monsters on the screen even though you know that in real life they are just actors. VR goes beyond movies, allowing you to be active *inside* the world you are watching—something you can't do with movies or TV. Because you decide where to go and how to act, virtual reality is considered to be interactive. You can interact with the VR world as if you were inter-acting with your friends and family—something you can't do with characters in a film. This interactivity heightens the ability of VR to make you believe you are somewhere you're not.

Robot Explorers

Thanks to VR, being in your bedroom doesn't stop you from running across the ocean floor or chasing alien star fighters. But what if VR were used to actually take you someplace that was real, like a museum, the inside of a volcano, or another continent?

Researchers have already thought of this and are using VR to take them to real places they couldn't otherwise get to. They wear the same VR gear, but instead of using VR software, which creates worlds out of computer commands, they use robots and video cameras.

The inside of a volcano is so hot a person would burn up there in only a few minutes. Robots, however, can be built to withstand temperatures as extreme as the heat of a volcano or the cold of the South Pole. These robots can be equipped with video cameras for eyes and small mechanical arms—sort of like *Star Wars*'s R2-D2. So far, two of these VR robots, which are only a few feet high, have been used to explore the Antarctic and the inside of a volcano.

The robot's video-camera eyes act just like the eyes of the researcher. Using satellite and cable transmission—which is used

In 1994, the Dante II robot explored inside Mt. Spurr, an active volcano near Anchorage, Alaska.→

to send regular TV pictures—the robot's eyes send video pictures back to the researcher's headset so that the researcher can see the scene in the same way he or she might see video images from a regular VR game. When the researcher turns his or her head, a tracking device in the VR helmet causes the robot to turn its head. When the researcher looks around, the robot looks around. Using the robot's eyes just like his or her own, the researcher can see everything he or she needs to see.

The robot's arm, which also transmits and receives data by cables and satellites, is linked to the researcher's dataglove, and all the movements the researcher makes are transmitted to the robot. When the researcher moves his or her arm forward, the robot does the same. When the researcher grabs for an object such as a rock or a piece of ice, the robot does, too. The robot is the researcher's

double, in a way. The real world of the robot becomes the virtual world of the researcher, and they share the same events and experiences, even though the researcher may be hundreds of miles away from the robot. Because the robot acts as his or her eyes, ears, and hands, the researcher can seemingly be in two places at once.

VR Museums

Going to other places via VR is not limited to out-of-the-way or dangerous parts of the world. A number of universities in the United States and Japan are creating museums where people can look at famous works of art in other countries without ever leaving their hometowns. They are building a virtual museum where people can stroll along at their leisure and look at different objects for as

long as they want. The interesting thing about this museum is that it isn't a place at all, it exists only on the computer. Unlike the Antarctic and volcano worlds, where robots make VR possible in real locations, the virtual museum will not be in a physical building that you could visit on your own if you were in the right city. Instead, it is only a piece of software, like a video game, and there is only one way to get to it: over the telephone lines.

An Egyptian temple in 3-D. This is based on an ancient Egyptian temple of Horus, the god of the sky.→

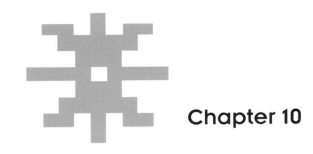

Chapter 10

Phone lines

are quickly becoming the most important way to get information from one place to another. Computers send data over these lines, faxes come over these lines, and it will only be a matter of time before TV programs and movies come over these lines, too. (The plan to put TV programs and videos on phone lines will lead to what is called the information superhighway.) There are even phone systems that allow you to attach a small video

Fiber-optic cables let us communicate around the world.

Phone calls will soon be replaced with video calls.

camera to your phone so that you can see who you are talking to on the other end.

These phone lines aren't exactly lines as we know them. They aren't made up of wires running from one place to another all over the world. Although they often do include wires, they primarily use such things as fiber-optic cables (which transmit light) and satellites (which transmit data signals from computers). All together these components form what is known as a telecommunications network.

Cyberspace

VR developers plan on using a telecommunications network to bring people together in places that don't really exist, like the virtual museum. People call these non-existent places cyberspace. You can't touch cyberspace or see it unless you are hooked up to a computer by a phone line. This idea might sound weird, but it will become clear as you read on.

In a way, talking on the phone is kind of like being in cyberspace. When you talk on a regular phone, you don't see the person at the other end. You know the person is there, but you only hear a voice. Let's say you are talking to a friend. As you are talking, you know what your friend looks like and you can make pictures of him or her in your mind, even though you can't see him or her at the moment. You can even picture the room your friend is in if you've been in that room before.

You and your friend are sharing a common environment and activity (your phone call), but you are in two different places. The thing that links you is a telecommunications network, which has connected the two of you over many miles and sent your voices up to satellites or along telephone wires and back again. This is not a link you can touch, though you probably use it every day without even thinking about it. It is not a physical link but a virtual link.

Sharing Experience From Separate Places

Now suppose that somewhere in between you and your friend someone places a computer with VR software on it. You might be in one town, your friend might be in another town, and the computer might be in a third town. Imagine that you and your friend have video game attachments to your phones that have joysticks and video screens like those on a

Nintendo® or Sega® machine. Then imagine that the actual game is located on the computer that is located in that third town. You and your friend decide that you want to play a game of chess (even though you're many miles apart), so you both call up the computer—in the same way that you would turn on your home video game—and you use that computer to play chess. Each of you sees the other, and you both see the board because the computer is generating images that make it appear that you are playing in the same room. Thus, you and your friend are playing together in cyberspace, and you are sharing the same experience from separate places.

Students from around the world can meet each other without leaving their own classrooms.

Chapter 11

Doing Business in Cyberspace

Companies

Companies everywhere find the idea of doing business in cyberspace fascinating. Many businesses have offices all around the world, and it is difficult and expensive for them to continually bring people from these offices together to discuss business plans. This is especially true in businesses where different people at separate locations work together to develop a single product. To show how difficult developing a product is without using VR, let's use a large fictional automobile company as an example. Let's call the company Car Maker X.

The Insanity virtual car is a combination of race car and luxury car.

As a virtual driver you can test a variety of driving conditions.→

Making Cars the Old Way

Car Maker X wants to build a new sports car. It will manufacture the car in the United States, but the group that is designing the actual body of the car is in Italy, and the people who are designing the car's interior are in Japan. The way things work today, the Italian and Japanese designers would have to send their drawings to one another and to the American manufacturers so that everybody would know what was being designed. If any group had a change, they would have to send those changes to the other groups. After each change was okayed, new drawings would have to be sent out. All this would take a great deal of time. In a company the size of Car Maker X, which employs one hundred thousand people and builds cars with thousands of parts, it would be an extremely long process. In fact, the time it takes a company to design a new car and then actually build it is between three and five years. Much of this time is spent trying to get everybody in different locations to agree on the various designs and drawings.

Making Cars With Virtual Reality

Now we'll insert a VR system into Car Maker X's design process. Car Maker X puts the design of its new car onto a computer, creating a virtual car. Like the video game that you and your friend play over the phone, this virtual car is on a computer that is separate from the offices in the United States, Italy, and Japan. Instead of traveling to one particular location, all the designers in these countries are outfitted with VR equipment. They all call one another up at a specific time. Then they call the computer where the virtual car is, just as you did when you called up the video game. When they are hooked up to the computer, they can all see the same virtual car.

Since everyone in the group is wearing VR gear, they can do all the things that are part of virtual reality. Using microphones that act as telephones, they can talk and listen to one another. They can also see the car, touch it, and walk around it. Even though they are in different parts of the world, separated by many thousands of miles, they are all looking at the exact same image. As they talk to one another (just as they do when they use regular phones), each person can point to the things that he or she would like to change and explain why. For example, one designer might feel that there needs to be more leg room in the

A futuristic car model designed in 3-D.→

driver's seat, while another designer might feel that the radio is too hard for the driver to reach. (You know how much easier it is to show somebody what you mean than to explain it over the phone or in a letter or fax.)

This entire meeting of people from Car Maker X is taking place in cyberspace. The moment they all disconnect from the phone lines, the car disappears—so to speak—and returns to its residence as a piece of software on the computer.

The really interesting thing about this meeting in cyberspace is that all the people can see one another. They don't see one another face-to-face, though. They see computer representations of one another (just as you see computer representations of aliens in VR games). Because the car is located in cyberspace, the people, too, have to enter cyberspace via the computer. To do

this, they have to create simulations of themselves inside the computer. This means that their images are generated by the computer from the movements that they make in their own offices. When they move their arms or walk around or look under the hood of the car, their virtual doubles do the same thing. Each designer can see what all the other designers are doing, and they can walk around as if they were all in the same room. This is done in a way that is similar to the way researchers control robot movements in dangerous places. But the virtual doubles in this case are not robots but accurate representations of the users themselves.

In VR, a driver can change the outside environment and the dimensions of the car's interior.

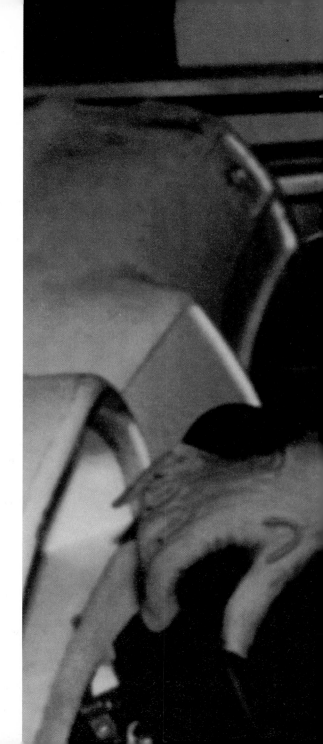

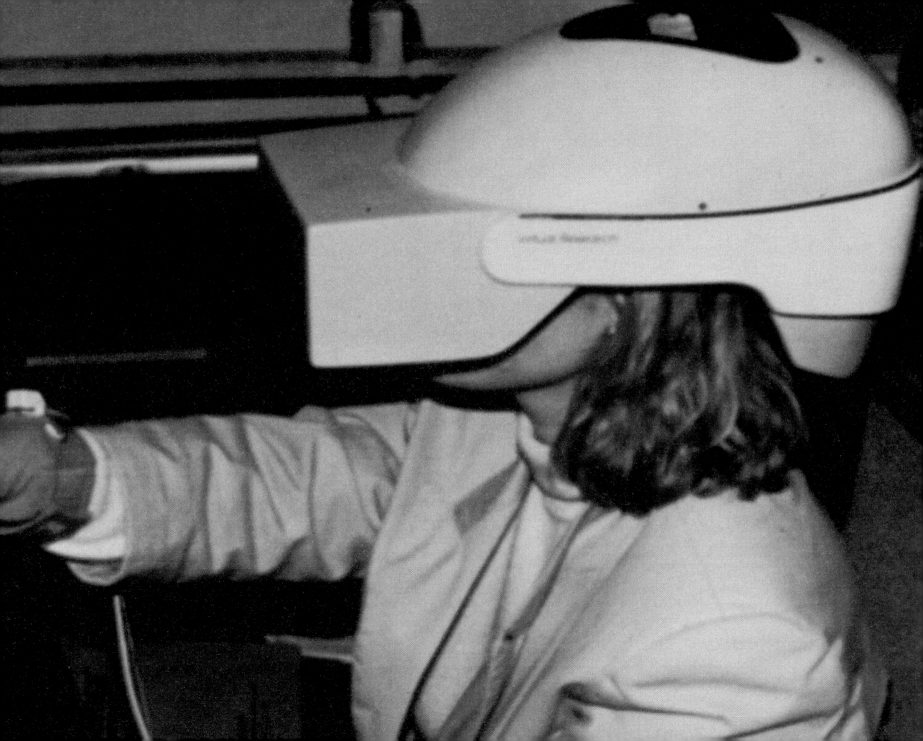

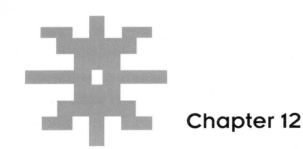

Chapter 12

Making New Friends in Virtual Reality

As shown in these composite pictures, you can play a game of virtual volleyball . . .

You have probably heard of pen pals. You might even have a pen pal. Pen pals are friends that communicate by writing letters back and forth to each other. They may have gotten each other's names from their schools or their parents, and they may live in different parts of the world. Pen pals exchange stories and jokes when they write to each other, and they also tell each other about their own families and how they live. Most pen pals have never met, but their friendships are as strong as if they lived on the same street.

. . . or a game of virtual basketball called "Jump Shot!"

Virtual Pen Pals

You can even change into a reptile in virtual reality. This composite picture shows what you would look like as a reptile.

Think of cyberspace friends as VR pen pals. You will meet somewhere in the telecommunications networks, perhaps only to play games. You may never meet in the real world, but you will still be able to interact with each other through your virtual doubles—just as the car designers interacted with one another. If you are playing virtual football, for instance, you will be able to see each other and hear each other and even tackle each other. Even though you will be alone when you do this, the VR gear is equipped with sensors that give you the sensation of grabbing somebody and wrestling around with him or her. (Remember the pressurized pads and air bags in the gloves? They will also be used

in full body suits—sort of like a VR uniform.)

Since you may be playing with kids that you've never met in real life, you may not ever know what they really look like, and they may not ever know what you look like. In cyberspace you will be able to

look like anything you want. For instance, one day you may decide you don't want to look like yourself. Instead, you may decide you want to look like a lizard. So you would reprogram the way your virtual double looks (this will be a simple thing to do in the future)

 76

You can play hackeysack in a virtual park, as shown in this composite.

pect them to. You may end up playing on a virtual basketball team with teammates who look like lions, tigers, and aliens.

Because people will be able to change their appearance in cyberspace, they will all be physically equal. No matter how big or how small you are, you will be able to change your size to fit in with everybody else's. If you are short, you will appear taller when you are playing virtual basketball. If you are tall but want to crawl into a small place, you will be able to make yourself the size of a hamster. In cyberspace, kids with handicaps who can't leave their houses will be able to play along with everyone else. Everyone will be able to play virtual baseball, football, basketball, or anything else because of the power of the technology. VR will let all kids do

so that it enters the virtual basketball court looking like a lizard instead of like you. It will still be your double, and will still move according to your movements, but it won't look like you anymore. It will look like a lizard that acts and talks like you.

Of course, your friends will also be able to transform their appearances. It will be fun to see the creative forms and shapes they choose when they disguise themselves in cyberspace. Be ready for lots of surprises because they will probably not look the way you ex-

You can even rock on a teeter-totter as does the boy in this composite picture.

Thousands of Worlds to Visit

Being in cyberspace will not mean that you are limited to playing one game. You will be able to enter and exit games whenever you please. Like the computer information services—called electronic bulletin boards—that are already in use today, there will be hundreds and even thousands of places for you to visit in cyberspace. You may choose to go to a virtual world where only games are played, or you may choose to go to a virtual museum. If you are having trouble with your math homework, you may be able to put on your equipment—or suit up—and go to a virtual world where math teachers can help you with your specific problems. You may be able to take a virtual field trip with your classmates—visit a laboratory in outer space, for example, or walk through a submarine. You may even decide to take your own virtual vacations when you get home from school, traveling to a desert island or a snow-peaked mountain. In the world of the future you may not even have to go to an actual school at all. You may just suit up and enter a virtual classroom, where you will learn with your friends in cyberspace.

To make your trips from the classroom to vacation worlds even easier, VR helmets may someday also allow you to look at a number of different things at once, like a room full of TV screens. You could watch what was happening on each screen, and if you wanted to join in the action, you could just touch a particular screen and then be sent into that virtual world—almost like jumping into an aquarium. Depending on what interested you the most, you could jump in and out of different worlds without taking a single step. You could spend all your time going from world to world, experiencing more things in a single day than you could in a whole year in real life.

Does this sound too good to be true? It shouldn't. All around the world many adults are already working at home without ever having to go into an office. They use telecommunications networks to talk to their coworkers and to send their work to their bosses. However, they occasionally do go into the office to meet with their coworkers in person, because it is always better to talk to people face-to-face than it is to communicate with them over phone lines.

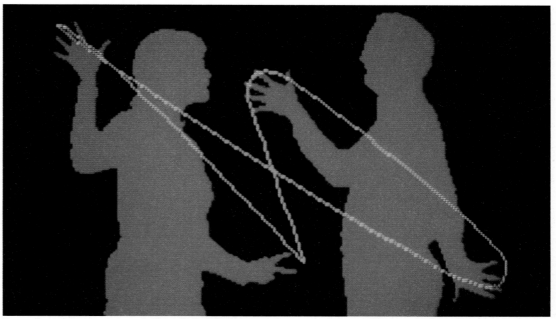

In cyberspace, you and a friend can make a cat's cradle just like the two players in this composite photo.

. . . Just Don't Forget the Real World

Perhaps the only negative part of VR is the temptation it poses to live your whole life in cyberspace. People might choose to spend all their time indoors in their VR suits and never bother to go outside or spend time with their friends in real life. Like kids who spend all their time in front of the TV, they would not get to experience the best parts of life—running around outside, for example, or hanging out with friends in the sunshine or simply reading a book. While VR may be close to real life, it will never replace real life.

Chapter 13

Virtual Reality— Today and Tomorrow

The big question in all of this is: When will it happen?

The big question in all of this is: When will it happen? A lot of it is happening today. The VR gear, including the headpieces and the datagloves, are already available with video games and in stores. Several toy manufacturers offer datagloves as replacements for video joy-sticks, so that you can actually see your hand in the video game, grabbing a magic object or a weapon. Some are also adding the headpiece to the games so that you can see the action on the screen from the inside.

In a virtual world you can paint the town red—or blue— just as the man in this composite photo is doing.

You Can Experience VR Today

For a little bit more money than you would spend on a regular video arcade game, you can experience virtual reality and participate in video games from the inside. Some of the arcade games located in malls in big cities enable you to do this, and some VR developers have their own amusement centers. You can strap on all the gear and then go to imaginary worlds where you battle with space aliens, or you can strap yourself into a cockpit and then fly an imaginary jet around the world.

Plans for the Future

The basic VR gear is being used right now, although developers are trying to make the gear cheaper and more lightweight. Someday it should

As seen in this composite, VR even lets you enter your favorite video game!

be as simple and easy to wear as a pair of glasses. The one aspect of VR that is still to come, however, is the development of all the virtual world computer programs that will be fun and interesting for you to use. It takes a lot of money to create these worlds, and right now many of them look more like computer graphics than like real life. Eventually VR worlds will be photorealistic (as realistic as pho-

tographs); they will seem to be just as real as our everyday world.

The telecommunications networks are already in place, and people use them everyday to get news and electronic messages. These networks are called on-line services and include the Internet, Prodigy®, CompuServe®, and America Online®. You may have heard of these, and your family or your school may have access to

Make your own virtual art as the artist does in this composite picture.

one of them. Regular users hang around the networks to discuss topics of interest with people they've never met in person. Often they find people on the networks who share their interests—such as music, sports, or stamp collecting—when they can't find people in their hometowns who do. On the networks there is a place for everyone and every interest.

The next step will be to link VR systems into these telecommunications networks. The governments of many big countries, especially the United States and Japan, hope to make this happen in the next few years. Vice President Al Gore has tried on a VR suit and entered a virtual world, and he believes that VR is one of the most important technologies of the future. Along with large companies and research labs, the government wants the power of VR to also be available to everyone who would like to use it.

It will take some time, but eventually it will happen. All the pieces are there—the gear, the hardware, the software, and the telecommunications networks. They just need to be hooked into one another. When this happens, VR will be as common as television. And the more common it is, the less expensive it will be. The same thing has already happened to electronic appliances such as personal computers and calculators.

An imaginary planet in 3-D, created on computer, can look as authentic as a real one. →

You will be able to create your own world with virtual reality programs.

Twenty years ago calculators cost almost $1000; today they cost as little as $2. When VR becomes more affordable, it will be in people's homes, offices, and schools. Virtual worlds, like video game software, will be created very quickly (think how many different video game cartridges there are for sale), and the choice of worlds will be almost endless. Many companies will offer different types of virtual worlds, and there will be computer programs that will let you create your own virtual worlds—worlds that you can design to your own specifications.

So get ready for virtual reality, where you can make almost anything happen. It will be limited only by your imagination and your interest in exploring new and exciting worlds. VR will be a tool for learning and a tool for fun, and you will have the ability to explore the world around you in ways no other generation of people before you could ever have dreamed possible.

See you in cyberspace!

*Gerry Marks created **his** own virtual world—a world with hang-gliding and cycling robots!*

How This Book Was Created

The technology that makes VR possible is expanding at a rapid pace. New improvements are being made almost every day. Some of the advances that have been made are in computer programming. A program is a set of instructions that allows you to operate the computer. Perhaps you are already familiar with some of these programs, such as WordPerfect® and Microsoft Word®. Just as these text programs enable the user to change fonts and type sizes and rearrange words, there are now graphic programs that enable the user to alter an image's size, color, shape, and texture, and even replace an entire image with a new one. Gerry Marks and the designer of this book, Heidi North, spent a lot of time working with the program called Adobe Photoshop® to create its illustrations.

The progress in technology has been so rapid that current programs will look ancient in a few years—or maybe even in a few months from now. How is this happening? Developers are continually working to create programs that are quicker and easier to use and that have higher resolution—the thing that helps images look sharper and more detailed. Most of the 3-D illustrations and some of the 2-D pictures found in this book have taken advantage of these remarkable advances in program technology. In the following paragraphs, we describe the detailed—yet fascinating—process through which Gerry created a few of these incredible illustrations.

The 3-D image of Venus on page 39 was taken from a CD-ROM entitled *Scientific American Library's The Planets,* produced by Byron Preiss Multimedia. The CD-ROM's programmers were able to create what is called a computerized walk-through. We should probably call it a drive-through since the user rides on the surface of Venus. The images are based on real information transmitted from NASA satellites. Gerry put two frames from this drive-through into Adobe Photoshop® and overlapped them to create a stereoscopic, or double image. This made the pictures three-dimensional. The picture appears tilted because of the uphill movement of the virtual vehicle you are supposed to be riding.

What makes the 3-D rendering of the White House on page 47 so special is its successful combination of two different VR programs, Virtus VR™ and Bryce. The picture of the White House was taken from Virtus VR™, a home-computer program. The clouds were taken from Bryce, a nature-rendering program. Most VR programs, such as Virtus VR™, sacrifice the detail of their images so the program can operate more quickly. But Bryce does the opposite: It favors detail over speed. The Bryce program uses extremely detailed scientific information to build incredibly realistic environments. Currently most VR programs don't use such complicated data, but they will as technology advances. Gerry added the MAC™ interface window so you would feel as if you were viewing it on your computer screen.

A collaborative effort by Gerry Marks and a company called Amusitronix made the 3-D image of the sci-fi robots on page 85 possible. Amusitronix provided Gerry with the different components of this picture: They gave him Bryce files containing its background environment and they created two robots. Gerry then made the images into a 3-D game interface. He simulated a VR game of the future especially for this book!

When I was a kid, my dad started one of the first computer companies in the United States. As his company grew, my dad made it a point to take my family to his office to show us the computers he was building. We would often play simple games like checkers against these computers, which were as big as refrigerators. That was almost thirty years ago, and those refrigerator-sized computers have come so far that the same type of computer can now fit on a chip the size of a fingernail. Even today's pocket calculators are many times more powerful than the big computers my dad worked on back then. But those huge electronic creatures in his office—full of blinking lights and wires, just like in old science fiction movies—were my first exposure to the world of computers and technology.

After graduating from college, I found that there was a lot of interesting work going on in computer technology that went beyond building smaller and more powerful computers. While most people were using computers for work, such as doing accounting or writing reports, I found a small group of people who were trying to do more interesting things, like making robots that could talk or creating special effects for movies. The special effects often looked so real that people couldn't always tell the difference between the computer picture and the real one. I started writing about these people and their work, and eventually became one of the few people who could make all this complicated technology easy to understand. I wrote hundreds of articles on this advanced type of computer technology, and even managed to write a few books along the way. In the process, I've been asked to speak in places around the world—from China to Chicago to London to Long Beach—about computers which can do more than just calculate numbers or produce reports.

My writing has also provided me with the opportunity to work with some of the companies that are trying to make computers more adventurous. I've consulted with IBM, the world's largest maker of computers, on the benefits of creating computers that can think, and I've worked with Universal Studios on plans to make virtual reality a main attraction at its theme parks.

In the past few years, I've written several books about technology, but this is the first one designed for people just getting interested in computers and what they can do. Many adults don't like to use computers simply because they don't understand them. But you and your friends are the first generation in world history to have computers as part of your everyday life. Most of you will use virtual reality in the years to come, just like your parents use stereos and microwave ovens today. Fifteen years ago, people didn't have CD players or microwaves, and today almost everyone has them. The same will be true of computer technologies like VR—eventually everyone will have them.

In the next fifteen years, who knows what will happen? There will be new technologies that we can't even imagine today. I'll probably still be writing about new technology. And you can be certain that you will be a part of it.

HP Newquist

HP Newquist's books include *The Brain Makers* (Prentice Hall), *Music & Technology* (Billboard Books), and *Emerging Technologies* (Lafferty Publications). His work has appeared in and been cited by publications such as *The Wall Street Journal, Barron's, Forbes, USA Today,* and *Newsweek.* He is a regular columnist for the magazines *Computerworld, The Virtual Reality Report,* and *Guitar*.

About the Illustrator

Gerry Marks's fascination with three-dimensional art began at a young age. He and his father enjoyed visits to the Hayden Planetarium in his native New York City. On one of these visits, his father bought him a star chart with an instructional book that included 3-D glasses. He would look at the book for hours, spellbound by the stars jumping out at him. Little did he know he would someday create his own three-dimensional art!

Although Marks's formal training was in music at the City University of New York and Columbia, his continued fascination with visual imagery led him to study the subject on his own. He actually taught himself how to create three-dimensional art. He then began silk-screen print-ing and successfully making 3-D images of his own. Eager to share his knowledge with others, Marks then taught silk-screen printing at Cooper Union in New York City.

In 1974, Marks moved from creating individual 3-D images to creating entire environments. Many of his environments—com-binations of art and science—have been displayed in museums throughout the country and around the world. His work has been shown in Boston, San Fran-cisco, Chicago, New York, and Japan. He has permanent dis-plays at the New York Hall of Sci-ence and The San Francisco Exploratorium, and is a popular speaker, addressing audiences from children to experts in related fields.

Marks has made 3-D videos for rock bands like Skid Row and the Rolling Stones and has fused his art with other media as well, including music, computer graphics, theater design, and photography. Currently he is working on a giant 3-D mural for a New York City subway station.

Marks has a philosophy about art that influences all his work. He genuinely wants people to think about the role time and space play in our perceptions. It is his hope that his work will inspire young people today—and in the future—to inquire about the way we see the world. He hopes that those who have read this book will be equally inspired to do so.